EXTREMELY INAPPROPRIATE
Dad Jokes

Disclaimer: Many of these jokes contain what could be considered vile or offensive language and/or content and are only intended for a mature audience. Reader (and listener) discretion is advised.

EXTREMELY INAPPROPRIATE
Dad Jokes

More Than 300 Hazardous Jokes, Sidesplitting Puns, and Hilarious One-Liners to Make You the Master of Questionable Comedy

JOE KERZ

Racehorse Publishing

Racehorse Publishing books may be purchased in bulk at special discounts for sales promotion, corporate gifts, fund-raising, or educational purposes. Special editions can also be created to specifications. For details, contact the Special Sales Department, Skyhorse Publishing, 307 West 36th Street, 11th Floor, New York, NY 10018 or info@skyhorsepublishing.com.

Racehorse Publishing™ is a pending trademark of Skyhorse Publishing, Inc.®, a Delaware corporation.

Visit our website at www.skyhorsepublishing.com.

10 9 8 7 6 5 4 3 2 1

Library of Congress Cataloging-in-Publication Data is available on file.

Cover photograph by Getty Images

Interior art credit: iStockphoto/Getty Images

ISBN: 978-1-63158-514-2
E-Book ISBN: 978-1-63158-516-6

Printed in the United States of America

INTRODUCTION

As a dad, you can always be counted on to find a way to effectively ruin a perfectly nice moment with a corny, sometimes dated, but never ill-conceived dad joke. You do this wherever and whenever the opportunity presents itself with unflinching consistency because . . . frankly . . . you love to annoy your family. When your kids were born, it quickly became your mission in life—your sole reason for being—to antagonize and torment them (and your significant other) with eye-rolling jokes and miraculously uncool puns.

But the jokes in this volume are definitely not suitable to tell your kids! Just when you were starting to get bored with your regular material and consider re-examining your repertoire, *Extremely Inappropriate Dad Jokes* swoops in to save the day!

This magnificent book will equip you with more groan-inducing jokes—and what's worse (for your audience) is that they're even more cringe-worthy than the last batch. Each of the jokes enclosed in this awe-inspiring reference is sure to evoke some sort of response. Almost none of these responses will be laughter, but that's the point, right? The more face-palming and head-shaking, the better.

This tell-all guide is the perfect companion for mastering the art of the dad joke and expanding upon your serious lack of humor. After all, dad jokes are no laughing matter.

JOKES

A wife decides to spruce up her sex life by buying some crotchless lingerie. Pleased with herself, she dons the lingerie and sits on the sofa in front of her husband, spread eagle.

"Are those crotchless undies?" he asks.

"Yes," she replies seductively.

"Thank goodness for that!" her husband exclaims. "I thought you were sitting on the cat!"

2.

A MAN SPENDS NINE MONTHS TRYING TO GET OUT OF A WOMAN AND THE REST OF HIS LIFE TRYING TO GET BACK IN.

3.

Why does Miss Piggy douche with honey?

Because Kermit likes sweet and sour pork.

4.

Two men were in the doctor's office. Each of them is to get a vasectomy.

The nurse comes into the room and tells both men "Strip and put on these gowns before going in to see the doctor to have your procedures done."

A few minutes later, she returns and reaches into one man's gown and proceeds to fondle and ultimately begins to masturbate him. Shocked as he is, he asks, "Why are you doing that?" She replies, "We have to vacate the sperm from your system to have a clean procedure."

The man, not wanting to be a problem and enjoying it, allows her to complete her task. After she is through, she proceeds to the next man.

She starts to fondle him as she had the previous man,

but then drops to her knees and proceeds to give him oral sex. The first man, seeing this, quickly responds, "Hey! Why is it that I get masturbated and he gets a blow job?"

The nurse simply replies, "That's the difference between Medicare and Private Health Coverage!"

What's the difference between a tire and 365 used condoms?

One is a Goodyear. The other is a great year.

4

6.

A MAN AND HIS WIFE WERE TRYING TO DECIDE WHAT TO DO ONE EVENING.

The man says, "We'll flip a coin. Heads I get tail, tails I get head!"

7.

A husband comes home to find his wife with her suitcases packed in the living room. "Where the hell do you think you're going?" he asks.

She replies, "I'm going to Las Vegas. You can earn $400 for a blow job there, and I figured that I might as well earn money for what I do to you free."

The husband thinks for a moment, goes upstairs, and comes back down with his suitcase packed as well. "Where do you think you're going?" the wife asks.

"I'm coming with you . . . I want to see how you survive on $800 a year!"

8.

WHY DO WOMEN HAVE ORGASMS?

Just another reason to moan, really.

9.

WHAT DO YOU CALL A GUY WITH A SMALL DICK?

Justin.

10.

What do you call a guy with a giant dick?

Phil.

11.

WHAT HAS A HUNDRED BALLS AND SCREWS OLD WOMEN?

Bingo.

12.

A wealthy man had three sons but didn't know which one should inherit the bulk of his estate. With his health failing he devised a plan to test their entrepreneurial skills with the winner being the one chosen to reign over the family's wealth upon his demise.

He gathered his sons and gave each of them a duck, telling them they must do the best they can to turn the duck into a profit by sale or trade.

Off they went with ducks under their arms. Son #1 went door to door, eventually selling the duck for $20 which was a substantial profit in those days.

Son #2 was a little more creative. He decided to sell raffle tickets and raised the princely sum of $40.

Son #3, not known for being a good student or for being particularly wise, was ambling along wondering what he was going to do when he met up with a local prostitute. She was quite interested in the duck so he said he would exchange it for a shag. With the deal done, she told him she had enjoyed it so much that if he did her again like that, he could have the duck back. Of course, being the young gentleman that he was, he was happy to oblige. Once they had finished round two he finished getting dressed, grabbed the duck, and headed off down the street with the duck

under his arm and a dopey smile on his face. He wasn't paying attention to where he was walking and he strayed into the path of a gent on horseback. #3 was knocked to the ground along with the duck who sustained a bruised beak and lost some feathers. Unfortunately, the bird was no longer able to fly and its quacking days were over.

The rider was very apologetic, and he knew the young man's father, so in a bid to make good for knocking them over he offered $50 as compensation, quickly mounting his horse and getting out of there.

The son picked up the duck and walked home.

Once the boys were all back home the father sat them down and asked what they had done and how much they had made.

Son #1 proudly stood and announced that he had gone door to door in a good part of the town and had sold his duck for $20.

Son #2, also proud of his effort, and knowing that son #3 still had his duck with him, stood and smiled and told his tale of selling raffle tickets and raising $40, sure that he would win.

Son #3 stood with his duck. His father asked "Son, what happened? You come back to me with the duck I sent you off with this morning. Did you do nothing?"

Son #3 replies, "On the contrary, I had an eventful and rewarding day, Father. I got a f**k for a duck, a duck for a f**k, fifty bucks for a f**ked duck, and I've still got the f**kin' duck!"

A mother is in the kitchen one day, preparing dinner for the family.

Her young daughter walks in and asks her, "Mommy, where do babies come from?"

The mother thinks for a while before deciding she ought to be honest with her daughter. She says, "Well honey, Mommy and Daddy fall in love and get married. One night they go into their bedroom, they kiss and hug, and then they have sex."

The daughter looks confused, so the mother says, "That means that Daddy puts his penis in Mommy's vagina. That's how you get a baby."

The daughter thinks for a moment and then seems to understand. Then she says, "Oh, I see. But the other night when I came into your room you had Daddy's penis in your mouth. What do you get when you do that?"

The mother replies, "Jewelry, my dear. Jewelry."

14.

WHAT'S LONG AND HARD AND FULL OF SEMEN?

A submarine.

15.

A doctor and his wife were arguing heatedly at breakfast. "You're not even that good in bed!" he shouted before storming off to work. By mid-morning, he decided his parting comment was uncalled for, so he sheepishly rang home to apologize. The phone rang for a long time before she answered.

"What took you so long to answer?" he asked.

"I was in bed," she replied.

"What were you doing in bed this late?"

"Getting a second opinion."

16.

Dad: Hey Son, want to hear a joke?

Son: Yeah.

Dad: Pussy.

Son: I don't get it.

Dad: Exactly!

17.

A husband and wife go back to the same hotel they stayed at on their wedding day for their 25th wedding anniversary.

As they reflect back on that magical night 25 years ago, the wife asks the husband, "When you saw my naked body what's the first you wanted to do?"

The husband replies, "Screw your brains out and suck your tits dry."

His wife then strips in front of him and asks, "What about now?"

The husband replies, "Looks like I did a great job!"

You can tell all you need to know about a person by whether they bring the banana to their mouth or their mouth to the banana.

19.

WHAT DO YOU CALL A MAN WHO CRIES WHILE HE MASTURBATES?

A tear jerker.

Son: Do you know what sexual position produces the ugliest children?

Dad: Go ask your mother.

21.

My wife just caught me blow-drying my erection and asked what the hell I was doing. . . .

Apparently, heating your dinner wasn't the right answer.

22.

HOW DO YOU MAKE A HORMONE?

Don't pay her.

23.

WHAT'S THE DIFFERENCE BETWEEN LOVE, TRUE LOVE, AND SHOWING OFF?

Spitting, swallowing, and gargling.

24.

A guy enters a bar carrying an alligator. He says to the patrons, "Here's a deal. I'll open this alligator's mouth and place my genitals inside. The gator will close his mouth for one minute, then open it, and I'll remove my unit unscathed. If it works, everyone buys me drinks."

The crowd agrees. The guy drops his pants and puts his privates in the gator's mouth. Gator closes mouth. After a minute, the guy grabs a beer bottle and bangs the gator on the top of its head. The gator opens wide, and he removes his genitals unscathed. Everyone buys him drinks.

Then he says, "I'll pay anyone who's willing to give it a try $100." After a while, a hand goes up in the back of the bar. It's a woman. "I'll give it a try," she says, "but you have to promise not to hit me on the head with the beer bottle."

25.

A construction worker came home just in time to find his wife in bed with another man. So, he dragged the man down the stairs to the garage and put his penis in a vise. He secured it tightly, super glued it shut, and removed the handle. Then he picked up a hacksaw.

The man, terrified, screamed, "Stop! Stop! You're not going to . . . to . . . cut it off, are you?"

The husband, with a horrible gleam of revenge in his eye, said, "Nope. You are. I'm going to set the garage on fire!"

26.

An old guy is sitting on a bus when a punk rocker gets on. The punk rocker's mohawk is red, green, yellow, and orange. He has feather earrings. When he sees the old man staring at him, the punk rocker says, "What's the matter, old man? Didn't you ever do anything wild when you were a young guy?"

The old guy says in reply, "Yeah. One time I screwed a peacock. I thought maybe you were my kid."

27.

A man is in a hotel lobby. As he runs to the front desk, he accidentally bumps into a woman and as he does, his elbow hits her breast. They are both quite startled. The man turns to her and says,

"Ma'am, if your heart is as soft as your breast, I know you'll forgive me."

She replies, "If your penis is as hard as your elbow, I'm in room 243."

28.

A man entered a restaurant and sat at the only open table. As he sat down, he knocked the spoon off the table with his elbow. A nearby waiter reached into his shirt pocket, pulled out a clean spoon, and set it on the table. The diner was impressed. "Do all the waiters carry spoons in their pockets?"

The waiter replied, "Yes. Ever since we had that efficiency expert out; he determined that 17.8% of our diners knock the spoon off the table. By carrying clean spoons with us, we save trips to the kitchen."

The diner ate his meal. As he was paying the waiter, he commented, "Forgive the intrusion, but do you know that you have a string hanging from your fly?"

The waiter replied, "Yes, we all do. Seems that the same efficiency expert determined that we spend too much time washing our hands after using the men's room. So, the other end of that string is tied to my penis. When I need to go, I simply pull the string to pull out my penis, go, and return to work. Having never touched myself, there is no need to wash my hands. Saves a lot of time."

"Wait a minute," said the diner, "how do you get your penis back in your pants?"

"Well, I don't know about the other guys, but I use the spoon."

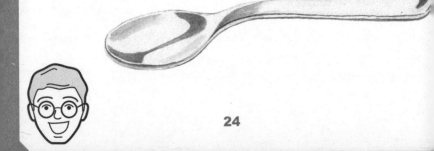

29.

Several years ago, Great Britain funded a study to determine why the head on a man's penis is larger than the shaft. The study took two years and cost over $1.2 million. The study concluded that the reason the head of a man's penis is larger than the shaft was to provide the man with more pleasure during sex.

After the results were published, France decided to conduct their own study on the same subject. They were convinced that the results of the British study were incorrect. After three years of research at a cost of an excess of $2 million, the French researchers concluded that the head of a man's penis is larger than the shaft to provide the woman with more pleasure during sex.

When the results of the French study were released, Australia decided to conduct their own study. The Aussies didn't really trust British or French studies.

So, after nearly three hours of intensive research and a cost of right around $120.00 (3 cases of beer), the Aussie study was complete. They concluded that the reason the head on a man's penis is larger than the shaft is to prevent your hand from flying off and hitting you in the forehead.

Last night, my wife and I were having Christmas dinner with her parents, grandparents, aunts/uncles, and a German neighbor who is a widow. We were talking about messing up while cooking meals and I mentioned the first time I cooked a turkey I cooked it upside down.

The neighbor was incredulous that I could make such a mistake and asked how I could possibly do this

when the breast would be round and make it diffi-
cult to get the turkey to not roll. I responded jokingly,
"Maybe I just like flat breasted turkeys."

My wife looked down at her chest. "Well now I feel
self-conscious. . . . Wait, is that why you always turn
me face down?"

A young couple took their two-year-old son to the
doctor. With some hesitation, they explained that,
although their little angel appeared to be in good
health, they were concerned about his rather small
penis. After examining the child, the doctor confi-
dently declared, "Just feed him pancakes. That should
solve the problem." The next morning, when the boy

arrived at breakfast, there was a large stack of warm pancakes in the middle of the table. "Gee, Mom," he exclaimed. "For me?"

"Just take two," his mother replied. "The rest are for your father."

32.

It was the mailman's last day on the job after 35 years of carrying the same mail through all kinds of weather to the same neighborhood.

When he arrived at the first house on his route, he was greeted by the whole family there, who congratulated him and sent him on his way with a big gift envelope.

At the second house they presented him with a big box of fine cigars.

The folks at the third house handed him a selection of terrific fishing lures.

At the fourth house he was met at the door by a strikingly beautiful woman in a revealing negligee. She took him by the hand, gently led him through the door (which she closed behind him), and led him upstairs to the bedroom, where she blew his mind with the most passionate love he had ever experienced. When he had had enough, they went downstairs where she cooked him a giant breakfast: eggs, potatoes, ham, sausage, blueberry waffles, and fresh-squeezed orange juice.

When he was truly satisfied, she poured him a cup of steaming coffee. As she was pouring, he noticed a dollar bill sticking out from under the cup's bottom edge.

"All this was too wonderful for words," he said, "but what's the dollar for?"

"Well," she said, "last night, I told my husband that today would be your last day, and that we should do

29

something special for you. I asked what to give you and he said, 'Screw him, give him a dollar.'"

Then the lady said, "The breakfast was my idea."

A father and son walk into a bar and the dad says to the son, "What do you want, fathead?" The son stumbles on his words and the father again says, "What do you want, fathead?" A lady close by asks, "Why do you keep calling your son fathead?"

He replies, "Well lady, there are 3 things a man has to have in his life to be successful. First, you got to have a big truck. See my truck over there? Biggest truck in the county. Second, you got to have a big house. See that house down the street? That's mine, the biggest house in the county. And thirdly, you have to have a tight pussy, and I had one . . . until this fathead came along."

34.

A preacher wanted to earn money for the building expansion program of his church. He had heard there was big money in horse racing, so he decided to purchase a horse and enter him in the races. However, at the local auction the going price for horses was too steep and the preacher ended up buying a donkey. The preacher figured he had the donkey, he might as well enter it in the race. The next day the donkey came in third. The racing form's headline the following day read, "Preacher's Ass Shows." The preacher

was so pleased with his donkey that he entered him the next day also. The donkey won. The newspaper's headline read, "Preachers Ass Out in Front."

However, the bishop was so upset with this type of publicity that he ordered the preacher not to enter the donkey in the races anymore. Then, the headlines read, "Bishop Scratches Preacher's Ass." This was too much for the bishop, and he ordered the preacher to get rid of the donkey. The preacher decided to give the animal to a nearby convent.

The next day's headlines read, "Nuns Have Best Ass in Town." The bishop fainted! He informed the nuns to get rid of the animal. So, they sold it to a farmer for $10.00. The next day the paper read, "Nuns Peddle Ass for Ten Bucks." They buried the bishop the next day. The paper read, "Too Much Ass Responsible for Bishop's Death."

35.

A couple on holiday in idyllic Capri were having some antipasto and wine overlooking a magnificent water-scape late one afternoon. At the adjacent table sat a very well-dressed man eating and drinking alone. The couple noticed that occasionally, every now and then, people would walk past and look at the well-groomed gent and smirk or giggle in his direction in a somewhat derisive manner. Each time it happened he lowered his head and looked ashamed.

Seeing that he looked despondent, the wife whispered to her husband and then asked the man if he would like to join them. Happily, he agreed, and they sat trading stories, drinking wine, and enjoying their surroundings. After a while, the couple mentioned that they had wit-nessed some people being somewhat rude to him and asked if they minded telling him what made him so sad.

He said, "Look, see that marina down there, with that

big yacht? That's mine. I built that yacht. Now I have a yacht-building business known the world over, but do they call me Guido the yachtbuilder? No they don't."

The couple were impressed but Guido continued, "See that villa on the hillside? I built that and many others like it. Do they call me Guido the house builder? No.

"Did you see the large church as you came into town? I built that, but do they call me Guido the church builder? No.

"But f**k one goat. . . ."

A lonely old spinster goes into an adult shop and is quietly looking around when a shop assistant approaches her and asks her if he could help her. She shyly

34

says that she is interested in one of those sex devices she heard about at bingo last week. The assistant takes her over to the display counter and begins to show her the range: "This one is latex, this one has a rotating head, this one is double ended," etc. "Is there any of these that interest you?" he asks.

The shy old spinster says, "They all look interesting . . . and I particularly like the look of that silver one over there."

The assistant then told her, "Sorry lady . . . that one is my thermos!"

I was in bed with a blind girl last night and she said that I had the biggest penis she had ever laid her hands on.

I replied, "You're pulling my leg."

38.

My girlfriend thinks that I'm a stalker.

Well, she's not exactly my girlfriend yet.

39.

Went for my routine check-up today and everything seemed to be going fine until he stuck his index finger up my backside!

Do you think I should change dentists?

40.

My wife has been missing for over a week now.

When I reported it to the police, they told me to prepare for the worst.

So, I went to Goodwill to get all of her clothes back.

41.

WHEN GUYS SAY, "SUCK IT," I ALWAYS REPLY WITH "SORRY, SMALL OBJECTS ARE A CHOKING HAZARD."

42.

A friend of mine has just told me he's getting it on with his girlfriend and her twin.

I asked, "How can you tell them apart?"

He replied,"That's easy. Her brother has a moustache."

43.

Condoms don't always guarantee that you'll have safe sex. . . .

For example, my friend was wearing one while having sex and got shot by the girl's boyfriend!

44.

The Red Cross just knocked at our door and asked if we could help towards the floods in Pakistan.

I said we would love to, but our garden hose only reaches the driveway.

45.

WHAT IS THE DIFFERENCE BETWEEN YOUR WIFE AND YOUR JOB?

After five years your job still sucks.

Why are hurricanes normally named after women?

When they come they're wild and wet, but when they go they take your house and car with them.

Why are penises the lightest things in the world?

Even thoughts can raise them.

48.

WHAT'S THE DIFFERENCE BETWEEN A HOOKER AND A DRUG DEALER?

A hooker can wash her crack and sell it again.

What's worse than waking up at a party and finding a penis drawn on your face?

Finding out it was traced.

50.

WHY DIDN'T THE TOILET PAPER CROSS THE ROAD?

It got stuck in a crack.

51.

What do you call an IT teacher who touches up his students?

A PDF file.

52.

How did the Burger King get the Dairy Queen pregnant?

He forgot to wrap his Whopper!

53.

What's the last thing Tickle Me Elmo receives before leaving the factory?

Two test-tickles.

54.

Do you know what 6.9 is?

A good thing screwed up by a period.

55.

What do a Rubik's cube and a penis have in common?

The more you play with them, the harder they get!

56.

How do you make a pool table laugh?

Tickle its balls.

57.

What does a perverted frog say?

"Rubbit!"

58.

What is the best pick-up line at a gay bar?

"May I push your stool in?"

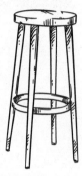

59.

What is the difference between a Genealogist and a Gynecologist?

A Genealogist looks up your family tree, whereas a Gynecologist looks up your family bush.

60.

WHAT'S GREEN AND SMELLS LIKE PORK?

Kermit the Frog's finger.

61.

What do a nearsighted gynecologist and a puppy have in common?

A wet nose.

62.

WHAT DO YOU CALL AN ITALIAN HOOKER?

A pasta-tute.

63.

Who was the world's first carpenter?

Eve, because she made Adam's banana stand.

64.

WHEN YOU HAVE A CLAP LIGHT IN YOUR BEDROOM, ROUGH SEX ALSO BECOMES A RAVE. . . .

65.

What's the process of applying for a job at Hooters?

They just give you a bra and say, "Here, fill this out."

When do you kick a midget in the balls?

When he is standing next to your girlfriend saying her hair smells nice.

What do electric trains and women's breasts have in common?

They were originally intended for children, but it's men who play with them the most.

68.

What's the best thing about dating homeless chicks?

You can drop them off anywhere.

69.

WHAT DID THE BLIND MAN SAY WHEN HE PASSED THE FISH MARKET?

"Good morning, ladies."

70.

I saw an attractive woman spank her child at McDonald's after he threw his fries on the ground. . . .

So I threw mine on the ground too!

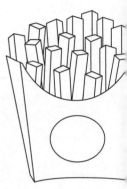

71.

What do tofu and a dildo have in common?

They are both meat substitutes!

72.

WHAT DO YOU CALL A DICTIONARY ON DRUGS?

Addictionary.

73.

What is Moby Dick's dad's name?

Papa Boner.

74.

I stubbed my toe while visiting my parents and, in pain, screamed, "MOTHERF****R!"

My dad then poked his head around the corner and said, "You rang?"

75.

How do you tell the difference between an oral and a rectal thermometer?

By the taste.

76.

HOW DOES A WOMAN SCARE A GYNECOLOGIST?

By becoming a ventriloquist!

77.

How is pubic hair like parsley?

You push it to the side before you start eating.

78.

How do you circumcise a hillbilly?

Kick his sister in the jaw.

79.

How is a woman like a road?

Both have manholes.

80.

WHAT DO GEORGE ZIMMERMAN, OJ SIMPSON, AND MASTURBATION HAVE IN COMMON?

Getting off once isn't enough for them.

81.

What do you call two guys fighting over a promiscuous woman?

Tug-of-whore.

82.

WHAT DID THE CANNIBAL DO AFTER HE DUMPED HIS GIRLFRIEND?

Wiped his butt.

83.

What does a 75-year-old woman have between her breasts that a 25-year-old doesn't?

Her navel.

84.

What did the toaster say to the slice of bread?

"I want you inside me!"

85.

What's the speed limit of sex?

68. At 69 you have to turn around.

86.

Why do vegetarians give good head?

Because they are used to eating nuts!

87.

WHAT'S THE DIFFERENCE BETWEEN A G-SPOT AND A GOLF BALL?

A guy will actually take time to search for a golf ball.

88.

What does the sign on an out-of-business brothel say?

"Beat it. We're closed."

89.

What do you call a woman who is paralyzed from the waist down?

Married.

90.

WHY DOES IT TAKE 100 MILLION SPERMS TO FERTILIZE ONE EGG?

Because they won't stop to ask directions.

91.

What's the difference between a pregnant woman and a lightbulb?

You can unscrew a lightbulb.

92.

What does one saggy boob say to the other saggy boob?

"If we don't get some support, people will think we're nuts."

93.

What's the best part about gardening?

Getting down and dirty with your hoes.

94.

How is a girlfriend like a laxative?

They both irritate the crap out of you.

95.

What do the Mafia and a vagina have in common?

One slip of the tongue, and you're in deep shit.

96.

WHAT DO YOU CALL THE USELESS PIECE OF SKIN ON A DICK?

The man.

97.

What's the difference between your boyfriend and a condom?

Condoms have evolved: they're not so thick and insensitive anymore.

98.

What's the difference between anal and oral sex?

Oral sex makes your day. Anal makes your hole weak.

99.

How is a push-up bra like a bag of chips?

As soon as you open it, you realize it's half empty.

100.

WHAT DID THE SANITARY NAPKIN SAY TO THE FART?

"You are the wind beneath my wings."

101.

Why can't you hear a psychologist using the bathroom?

Because the "p" is silent!

102.

What's better than roses on your piano?

Tulips on your organ.

103.

WHAT'S THE DIFFERENCE BETWEEN BEING HUNGRY AND BEING HORNY?

Where you put the cucumber.

104.

What do you call two lesbians in a closet?

A liquor cabinet.

105.

What do girls and noodles have in common?

They both wiggle when you eat them.

106.

WHAT'S THE WORST THING ABOUT DATING A BLONDE?

If you don't know what hole to put it in, neither does she.

107.

Did you hear about the cannibal that made a bunch of businessmen into chili?

I guess he liked seasoned professionals.

108.

What do you call a lesbian dinosaur?

A lickalotopuss.

109.

HOW IS A WOMAN LIKE A CONDOM?

Both spend more time in your wallet than on your dong.

110.

WHAT IS THE RECIPE FOR HONEYMOON SALAD?

Lettuce alone without dressing.

111.

What's long, hard, and erects stuff?

A crane!

112.

Why is it so hard for women to find men that are sensitive, caring, and good-looking?

Because all those men already have boyfriends.

113.

What are the three shortest words in the English language?

Is it in?

114.

Why do women rub their eyes when they get up in the morning?

They don't have balls to scratch.

115.

WHAT DID THE BANANA SAY TO THE VIBRATOR?

"Why are YOU shaking? She's going to eat me!"

116.

WE NEVER TRULY GROW UP . . . WE JUST GET BETTER SWING SETS!

117.

What kind of bees make milk?

Boo-Bees.

118.

**What do you call a party with
a hundred midgets?**

A little get together.

119.

**WHEN SOMEONE SAYS,
"YOU SUCK," REPLY WITH
"NOT FOR FREE."**

The look on their face is
always priceless!

120.

What did Cinderella do when she got to the ball?

She gagged.

121.

Daughter: Mom, how do you get Bill from William?

Mom: You change the W to a B.

Daughter: How do you get Bob from Robert?

Mom: You change the R to a B.

Daughter: Then how do you get Dick from Richard?

Mom: You ask him nicely.

122.

WHAT GOES IN HARD AND DRY, BUT COMES OUT SOFT AND WET?

Chewing gum.

123.

Why doesn't Santa Claus have any children?

Because he only comes once a year, and it's down your chimney.

124.

Why isn't there a pregnant Barbie doll?

Because Ken came
in another box.

125.

WHAT DID THE LEPER SAY TO THE PROSTITUTE?

"Keep the tip!"

126.

WHAT IS THE DIFFERENCE BETWEEN A CLEVER MIDGET AND A VENEREAL DISEASE?

One is a cunning runt, and the other is a running cunt.

127.

What's the difference between a bag of coke and a baby?

Eric Clapton would never let a bag of coke fall out the window.

128.

What's the difference between a hockey player and a hippie chick?

The hockey player takes a shower after three periods.

129.

WHAT DO YOU CALL TWO LARGE PEOPLE TALKING?

A heavy discussion.

130.

What's the difference between a gay man and a refrigerator?

The refrigerator doesn't fart when you take your meat out.

131.

WHAT DO YOU CALL AN EXPERT FISHERMAN?

A master baiter.

132.

What's the difference between a girl and a washing machine?

When a guy dumps a load in the washing machine, it doesn't follow him around.

133.

What's the best thing about a gypsy on her period?

When you finger her, you get your palm red for free.

134.

Who's the biggest hoe in history?

Ms. Pac-man, because for 25 cents she swallows
balls until she dies.

135.

DON'T YOU HATE IT WHEN YOU BUY NEW SOCKS AND YOU GET ALL THAT ANNOYING SOCK FLUFF . . . ?

Especially on your dick.

136.

WHAT DO YOU CALL A CHEAP CIRCUMCISION?

A rip-off.

137.

Did you hear about the celebrity murderer?

He was shooting for the stars.

138.

When a girl uses her bra as a pocket, what do you call her boobs?

Utilititties.

139.

WHY IS BEING IN THE MILITARY LIKE A BJ?

The closer you get to discharge, the better you feel.

140.

Why can't Jesus play hockey?

He keeps getting nailed into the boards.

141.

WHAT DID THE LETTER O SAY TO Q?

"Dude, your junk is hanging out."

142.

WHAT DO YOU CALL A NUN IN A WHEELCHAIR?

Virgin Mobile.

143.

What do you see when the Pillsbury Dough Boy bends over?

Doughnuts.

144.

What do you get when you mix LSD and birth control?

A trip without the kids!

145.

How do you know you have a high sperm count?

Your girlfriend has to chew before she swallows.

146.

TEACHER: JOHNNY, CAN YOU USE THE WORD "DICTATE" IN A SENTENCE?

Johnny: Annie said my dictate good!

147.

MY MIDGET FRIEND GOT THROWN OUT OF THE NUDIST COLONY BECAUSE HE KEPT GETTING IN EVERYONE'S HAIR.

148.

Maybelline claims to make eyelashes look three times longer. . . .

I think they should start making condoms!

149.

WHAT DO YOU CALL CRYSTAL CLEAR URINE?

1080pee.

150.

WHY WAS THE GUITAR TEACHER ARRESTED?

For fingering A minor.

151.

Did you hear about the guy who died of a Viagra overdose?

They couldn't close his casket.

152.

Why don't orphans play baseball?

They don't know where home is.

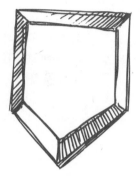

153.

Why wasn't Jesus born in the USA?

Because God couldn't find three wise men and a virgin.

154.

**I just caught a glimpse of my wife
wearing her sexy underwear.
This can only mean one thing. . . .**

Today is laundry day.

155.

WHY DID THE WALRUS GO TO THE TUPPERWARE PARTY?

Because he wanted to find a tight seal.

156.

What do Princess Diana and Pink Floyd have in common?

Their last big hit was the wall.

157.

What does it mean when your boyfriend is in your bed gasping for breath and calling your name?

You didn't hold the pillow down long enough.

158.

HIM: DID YOU CUM?

Her: Yes . . . to the realization that this was a mistake.

159.

What do you call an artist with a brown finger?

Piccassole.

160.

I told my friend that I made $500 a month selling dog poop.

He said, "That's gross!"

I said, "No, that's net."

161.

WHAT'S 72?

69 with three people watching.

162.

What three words will ruin a man's ego?

"Is it in?"

163.

What's the difference between your dick and a bonus check?

Someone's always willing to blow your bonus.

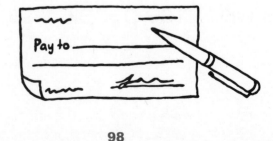

164.

WHAT'S THE DIFFERENCE BETWEEN A WOMAN WITH PMS AND A TERRORIST?

You can negotiate with a terrorist.

165.

What's an adult actress's favorite drink?

7 Up in cider.

166.

How do you embarrass an archaeologist?

Give him a used tampon and ask him which period it came from.

167.

HOW IS SEX LIKE A GAME OF BRIDGE?

If you have a great hand, you don't need a partner.

168.

HOW IS LIFE LIKE A PENIS?

Your girlfriend makes it hard.

169.

What four letter word that ends in "k" means the same as intercourse?

Talk.

170.

What did the hurricane say to the coconut tree?

"Hold on to your nuts, this ain't no ordinary blow job."

171.

What do you call balls on your chin?

A dick in your mouth!

172.

Doctor: Do you engage in regular physical activity?

Man: Does sex count?

Doctor: Yes, sex counts.

Man: Then no, none at all. . . .

173.

WHAT DID THE PENIS SAY TO THE VAGINA?

"Don't make me come in there!"

174.

What's the difference between a pickpocket and a peeping tom?

One snatches your watch. The other watches your snatch.

175.

How do you make your girlfriend scream during sex?

Call and tell her about it.

176.

What's warm, wet, and pink?

A pig in a hot tub.

177.

WHY WAS THE TWO-PIECE SWIMSUIT INVENTED?

To separate the hairy from the dairy.

178.

WHAT'S ANOTHER NAME FOR A VAGINA?

The box a penis comes in.

Oranges are actually male or female. . . .

If it squirts in your eye without warning, it's a male. If it's bitter for no reason, it's a female.

180.

What should you do if your girlfriend starts smoking?

Slow down. And possibly use a lubricant.

181.

WHY IS SPERM WHITE AND PEE YELLOW?

So a man can tell if he's coming or going.

182.

I NICKNAMED MY DONG "COIN FLIP" BECAUSE IT'S ALWAYS GETTING EITHER HEAD OR TAIL.

183.

LIFE WITHOUT WOMEN WOULD BE A PAIN IN THE BUTT, LITERALLY.

184.

Life is like toilet paper: you're either on a roll or taking crap from some asshole.

185.

The only way you'll ever get laid is if you crawl up a chicken's butt and wait.

186.

Kitchen sex: Probably my only chance to get laid on an island.

187.

Crowded elevators smell different to midgets.

188.

WHAT DO LIFESAVERS DO THAT A MAN CAN'T?

Come in eight flavors.

189.

What do cow pies and cowgirls have in common?

The older they get the easier they are to pick up.

190.

HOW CAN YOU TELL A SUMO WRESTLER FROM A FEMINIST?

A Sumo wrestler shaves his legs.

191.

Doctor: "I have some bad news for you. You really have to stop masturbating."

Man: "Oh my God, doc! Why?!?"

Doctor: "I'm trying to examine you."

192.

Ever have sex while camping?

It's very intents!

193.

What is the difference between Michael Jackson and a grocery bag?

One is made of plastic and is dangerous for children to play with. The other is used to carry groceries.

194.

What is the new O.J. website address?

/ / \ Esc (slash slash backslash escape)

195.

WHAT'S GOT FOUR LEGS AND ONE ARM?

A Rottweiler.

196.

DID YOU HEAR ABOUT THE 150 LB. MAN WHO HAD 75 LB. TESTICLES?

He was half nuts!

197.

What do you call it when a blonde is grabbing at air?

Collecting her thoughts.

198.

WHAT IS THE DIFFERENCE BETWEEN EROTIC AND KINKY?

Erotic is using a feather. Kinky is using the whole chicken.

199.

How are tornadoes and marriage alike?

They both begin with a lot of sucking and blowing, and in the end, you lose your house.

200.

What gets longer when pulled, inserts neatly in a hole, and works best when jerked?

A seatbelt.

201.

Why do men like big tits and tight pussy?

Because they've got big mouths and little dicks.

202.

Why do men name their penis?

They like to be on a first name basis with the one making most of their decisions.

203.

WHAT IS THE DIFFERENCE BETWEEN SNOWMEN AND SNOWWOMEN?

Snowballs.

204.

WHY DO ONLY **30%** OF MEN GET INTO **HEAVEN?**

If it were more, it would be Hell.

205.

What do you call two skunks that are 69ing?

Odor eaters.

What is the difference between oooooooh and aaaaaaah?

About three inches.

Why don't women have any brains?

Because they don't have penises to keep them in.

208.

WHAT TWO THINGS IN THE AIR CAN MAKE A WOMAN PREGNANT?

Her feet!

209.

Why can't Miss Piggy count to 70?

Because she gets a frog in her throat at 69.

210.

What do elephants use for tampons?

Sheep.

211.

WHERE DOES AN IRISH FAMILY GO ON VACATION?

A different bar.

212.

I WAS MASTURBATING TODAY, AND MY HAND FELL ASLEEP. . . . THAT'S GOT TO BE THE ULTIMATE REJECTION.

213.

What would you call it when an Italian has one arm shorter than the other?

A speech impediment.

214.

What does it mean when the flag at the Post Office is flying at half-mast?

They're hiring.

215.

What do smoking a cigarette and eating someone out have in common?

The closer you get to the butt, the worse it tastes.

216.

Why do drivers education classes in redneck schools only use the car on Mondays, Wednesdays, and Fridays?

Because on Tuesday and Thursday, the Sex Ed class uses it.

217.

What's the difference between a Southern zoo and a Northern zoo?

A Southern zoo has a description of the animal on the front of the cage, along with a recipe.

How do you get a sweet little 80-year-old lady to say "shit"?

Get another sweet little 80-year-old lady to yell "BINGO!"

What's the difference between a Northern fairytale and a Southern fairytale?

A Northern fairytale begins, "Once upon a time . . ."
A Southern fairytale begins, "Y'all ain't gonna believe this shit . . ."

220.

WHAT IS THE QUICKEST WAY TO CLEAR OUT A MEN'S RESTROOM?

Say, "Nice dick."

221.

How do you know you're leading a sad life?

When a nymphomaniac tells you, "Let's just be friends."

222.

What do you get when you cross Billy Ray Cyrus and a yeast infection?

An itchy, twitchy twat.

223.

ARE BIRTH CONTROL PILLS DEDUCTIBLE?

Only if they don't work.

224.

Why don't bunnies make noise when they make love?

Because they have cotton balls.

225.

WHY DO JEWISH MEN GET CIRCUMCISED?

Because Jewish women won't touch anything unless it's 20% off.

226.

What do gay men call hemorrhoids?

Speed bumps.

227.

WHEN DOES A CUB BECOME A BOY SCOUT?

When he eats his first Brownie.

228.

HOW DOES A SCOTSMAN FIND A SHEEP IN TALL GRASS?

Very satisfying.

229.

What do you call an Alabama farmer with a sheep under each arm?

A pimp.

230.

What do you get when you cross an owl and a rooster?

A cock that stays up all night.

231.

WHAT DO YOU CALL A NINETY-YEAR-OLD MAN WHO CAN STILL MASTURBATE?

Miracle Whip.

An autopsy professor was giving an introductory lecture to a class of students. Standing over a corpse, she addressed the class: "There are two things you need to make a career in medical forensics. First, you must have no fear."

Having said that, she shoved her finger up the corpse's anus and licked it.

"Now, you must do the same," she told the class.

After a couple minutes of uneasy silence, the class did as instructed.

"Second," the professor continued, "you must have an acute sense of observation. For instance, how many of you noticed that I put my middle finger up this man's anus, but licked my index finger?"

233.

Women who don't cook, clean, or suck dick always ask, "Where are all the good men?"

The good men just finished eating dinner and they're relaxing in a clean house about to get their dick sucked.

234.

Almost every hand you have ever shaken has had a dick in it.

A trucker who's been out on the road for two months stops in a brothel. He walks straight up to the madam, drops $500, and says, "I want your ugliest woman and a grilled cheese sandwich."

The madam is astonished. "But sir, for that kind of money you could have one of my prettiest ladies and a three-course meal!"

The trucker replies, "Listen darlin', I'm not horny, I'm just homesick!"

236.

Three little old ladies are sitting on a park bench, feeding the birds, when a man comes by and flashes them all.

The first two little old ladies have a stroke . . . but the third little old lady couldn't quite reach!

237.

An elephant and a camel are talking at a zoo.

Elephant: Why do you have titties on your back?

Camel: That's funny, coming from the guy with a dick on his face!

238.

I had a visitor one night.

He explored my body, licked, sucked, swallowed, and had his fill.

Once satisfied, he left. I was hurt.

Damn mosquito!

239.

When it's stiff, you stick it in. It goes in dry and comes out wet. The longer it's in, the stronger it gets. It comes out dripping and starts to sag. It's not what you think. . . .

It's just a tea bag.

240.

How to please a woman: Love her, die for her, take her to dinner, miss the game for her, buy her jewelry, and be interested in what she has to say.

How to please a man: Show up naked. With beer.

241.

My boyfriend doesn't know that I put a dollar in an envelope for every time he makes me orgasm, and that's all I'm spending on him for Christmas.

So far he's getting a McFlurry. . . .

242.

The best curse: May the fleas of a thousand camels infest the crotch of your enemy, and may their arms be too short to scratch!

243.

Wife: Damn, the rain got me all wet!

Husband: Really? You get turned on by the weirdest things. . . .

244.

A dick has a sad life: His hair is a mess, his family is nuts, his next-door neighbor is an asshole, his best friend is a pussy, and his owner beats him regularly.

245.

Guy: Can I buy you a drink?

Girl: Sorry, but alcohol is bad for my legs.

Guy: Oh, do they swell?

Girl: No. They spread.

246.

A couple is having sex when she looks at him and says, "Make love to me like in the movies."

So he f**ks her in the ass, pulls out, and comes all over her face and in her hair.

Apparently, they don't watch the same movies. . . .

247.

What do a clitoris, an anniversary, and a toilet have in common?

Men usually miss all three!

141

248.

MONDAY MUST BE A MAN. . . .
It comes too quickly!

A professor told dirty jokes in class, and the women decided to protest it. They all decided that the next time the professor started telling dirty jokes in class, they would all leave in protest.

Somehow the professor heard about the plan. So, at the beginning of the next lecture, he started out with: "In Sweden, a prostitute makes $2000 a night . . ."

All the women immediately stood up and started to leave the classroom.

The professor shouted after them, "Where are you going? The plane to Sweden doesn't leave till the day after tomorrow!"

Two boys are having an argument:

Boy 1: Shove off!

Boy 2: No, you shove off!

Boy 1: If I wanted my comeback, I would have wiped it off your mom's chin!

251.

A hard-of-hearing elderly man is going to the doctor and is accompanied by his wife:

Nurse: Alright, the doctor would like a urine sample, a stool sample, and a sperm sample.

Man: What did she say?

Wife: They want your underwear!

252.

Wife: Darling, do I please you in bed?

Husband: Yes, I love that trick you do with your mouth.

Wife: What trick?

Husband: The one where you shut the f**k up and go to sleep!

253.

I met a prostitute who said she'd do anything for $50. . . .

Guess who got his front porch repainted!

254.

What do a pizza delivery guy and a gynecologist have in common?

They both have to smell it, but they don't get to eat it!

255.

What's 6 inches long, 2 inches wide, and drives women wild?

A $100 bill

256.

WHAT'S LONG AND HARD AND HAS CUM IN IT?

A cucumber

257.

Girl: Hey, what's up?

Boy: If I tell you, will you sit on it?

WHY DO MEN GET THEIR GREAT IDEAS IN BED?

Because they're plugged into a genius!

**A red head tells her blonde sister:
"I slept with a Brazilian"**

The blonde replies,
"Oh my gosh, you slut! How many is a brazilian?!"

260.

What three great kings are known for bringing peace and happiness into people's lives?

Smo-King, Drin-King, and F*c-King

261.

What did the elephant ask the naked man?

"Hey that's cute, but can you breathe through it?"

WHAT'S THE DIFFERENCE BETWEEN ROAST BEEF AND PEA SOUP?

Anyone can roast beef, but no one can pea soup!

If a firefighter's business can go up in smoke and a plumber's job go down the drain, can a hooker get laid off?

264.

What's the difference between a nail stylist and a hair stylist?

One does hand jobs and the other does blow jobs!

265.

WHAT DO YOU GET WHEN YOU CROSS A DONKEY AND AN ONION?

A piece of ass that will bring a tear to your eye.

266.

Two men visit a prostitute. The first man goes into the bedroom. Ten minutes later he comes out and says, "Heck, my wife is better than that."

The second man goes into the bedroom. He also comes out ten minutes later and says, "You're right. Your wife is better than that!"

267.

A little boy kills a butterfly, and his dad says, "No butter for two weeks!"

Later, the boy kills a honeybee, and his dad says, "No honey for two weeks!"

Then, the mom kills a cockroach. The little boy turns to the dad and says, "Are you going to tell her, or should I?"

268.

When three people have sex, it's called a threesome.

When two people have sex, it's called a twosome.

Now I know why they call you handsome!

269.

I got kicked out of the hospital. . . .

Apparently, the sign that said "Stroke patients here" meant something completely different than what I thought!

270.

GIRLS HAVE MAGIC POWERS: THEY GET WET WITHOUT WATER, BLEED WITHOUT INJURY, AND MAKE BONELESS THINGS HARD!

271.

"Give it to me!" she yelled. "I'm soaking wet, give it to me now!"

She could yell all she wanted, I wasn't giving her the umbrella.

272.

A mom is cleaning her 12-year-old son's bedroom and finds a load of bondage gear and a fetish magazine. She asks her husband, "What do I do?"

Her husband replies, "I'm not sure, but whatever you do, don't spank him!"

273.

WHAT DO YOU CALL KIDS BORN IN WHOREHOUSES?

Brothel sprouts.

274.

**The sex position known as 69
has now been changed to 96....**

Due to the economy, the price of eating out
has gone up!

275.

**Boy: Want to hear a joke about my penis?
Never mind, it's too long!**

Girl: Want to hear a joke about my vagina?
Never mind, you'll never get it!

276.

WHAT DO YOU HAVE WHEN YOU HAVE TWO LITTLE BALLS IN YOUR HAND?

A man's undivided attention.

277.

Why are men like cars?

Because they never check to see if anyone is coming before pulling out!

Man: We should make a sex tape!

Wife: Yes, let's do it!

Wedding photographer: That's not really what I'm here for. . . .

You wanna hear a dirty joke?

A boy in a white shirt fell in the mud.

You wanna hear a dirtier joke?

He got back up and fell back down in the mud.

You wanna hear a clean joke?

He took a bath with Bubbles.

You wanna hear the dirtest joke so far?

Bubbles is the girl next door.

280.

HOW CAN YOU TELL WHEN AN AUTO MECHANIC JUST HAD SEX?

One of his fingers is clean.

281.

A guy goes to the store to buy condoms. The cashier asks him, "Do you want the bag?"

The man replies, "No, she isn't that ugly!"

282.

The kindergarten class had a homework assignment to find out about something exciting and relate it to the class the next day. When the time came for the little kids to give their reports, the teacher was calling on them one at a time. She was reluctant to call upon

Little Johnny, knowing that he sometimes could be a bit crude. But eventually his turn came.

Little Johnny walked up to the front of the class, and with a piece of chalk, made a small white dot on the blackboard, then sat back down. Well the teacher couldn't figure out what Johnny had in mind for his report on something exciting, so she asked him just what that was.

"It's a period," reported Johnny.

"Well, I can see that," she said, "but what is so exciting about a period?"

"Well, I don't know," said Johnny, "but this morning my sister said she missed one. Then Daddy had a heart attack, Mommy fainted, and the man next door started freaking out!"

The teacher asks little Johnny to use the word "definitely" in a sentence.

Little Johnny replies, "Teacher, do farts have lumps in them?"

The teacher says, "Of course not, Johnny."

To which Johnny replies: "Then I have definitely shit my pants."

One day, Little Johnny's teacher, Miss Figpot, asked the class if they could name some things you can suck.

"Ice cream, ma'am!" Little Mary answered.

"Good, Mary," Miss Figpot said. "Anyone else?"

"How about a lollipop?" said Steven.

"Very good, now it's your turn, Johnny!", the teacher said.

Little Johnny, sitting at back, then answered, "A lamp!"

The teacher and all of the students wondered about his answer. The teacher asked him, "Johnny, why do you think one can suck a lamp?"

"Last night when I passed my parents room," Little Johnny answered, "I heard my mom say, 'Turn off the lamp, honey, and let me suck it.'"

285.

**What's the quickest way to lose
190 pounds of ugly fat?**

Divorce him.

286.

A man is driving up a steep,
narrow mountain road. A woman is
driving down the same road. As they
pass each other, the woman leans out
of the window and yells, "PIG!"

The man immediately leans out of his window and
replies, "BITCH!"

They each continue on their way, and as the man rounds the next corner, he crashes into a pig in the middle of the road and dies.

If only men would listen.

287.

AFTER HEARING A PICK-UP LINE:

Woman: "I like your approach, now let's see your departure."

288.

"Honey," said a husband to his wife, "I invited a friend home for supper."

"What? Are you crazy? The house is a mess, I haven't been shopping, all the dishes are dirty, and I don't feel like cooking a fancy meal!"

"I know all that."

"Then why did you invite a friend for supper?"

"Because the poor fool's thinking about getting married."

289.

Larry gets home late one night and his wife, Linda, asks, "Where in the hell have you been?"

Larry replies, "I was out getting a tattoo."

"A tattoo?" she frowned. "What kind of tattoo did you get?"

"I got a one hundred dollar bill on my privates," he said proudly.

"What the hell were you thinking?" she said, shaking her head in disdain. "Why on earth would an accountant get a hundred dollar bill tattooed on his privates?"

"Well, one, I like to watch my money grow. Two, once in a while I like to play with my money. Three, I like how money feels in my hand. And, lastly, instead of you going out shopping, you can stay right here at home and blow a hundred bucks anytime you want."

George had responded to a call from his lawyer, insisting that they meet at once. He arrived at his lawyer's firm and was ushered into his office.

"Do you want the bad news first or the terrible news?" the lawyer asked.

"Well, if those are my choices, I guess I'll take the bad news first."

"Your wife found a picture worth a half-million dollars."

"That's the bad news?" George was stunned. "If you call that bad, I can't wait to hear the terrible news."

"The terrible news is that it's of you and your secretary."

291.

Two guys are sitting on a bar stool. One starts to insult the other one. He screams, "I slept with your mother!"

The bar gets quiet as everyone listens to see what the other guy will do.

The first again yells, "I SLEPT WITH YOUR MOTHER!"

The other says, "Go home, Dad, you're drunk."

292.

A couple is going to an art gallery. They find a picture of a naked women with only her privates covered with leaves. The wife doesn't like it and moves on but the husband keeps looking.

The wife asks, "What are you waiting for?"

The husband replies, "Autumn."

Three guys go on a skiing trip together.

When they get to the ski lodge there aren't enough rooms, so they have to share a bed.

In the middle of the night, the guy on the right side of the bed wakes up and says, "Wow, I had this mad dream I was getting a hand job."

The guy on the left side of the bed has also woken up, and says that he's had the same dream, too.

The guy in the middle says, "Wow that's funny, I dreamed I was skiing."

294.

Unexpected sex is a great way to be woken up. . . .

If you're not in prison.

295.

One day, a little boy and a little girl are fighting about the differences between the sexes, and which one is better.

After much arguing back and forth, the boy drops his pants and says, "Here's something I have that you'll never have."

The little girl is annoyed and upset by this, as what the boy says is obviously true. So she runs home to her mom, crying.

A short time later, she comes running back with a smile on her face. She goes to the boy, drops her pants, and says, "My Mommy says that with one of these, I can have as many of those as I want!"

296.

A man walks into a bar and orders ten shots of Jägermeister.

The bartender says, "Wow, that's a lot. Are you celebrating?"

The man replies, "Yes! My first blowjob!"

The bartender says, "Oh, congratulations! But if you don't mind me asking, why ten shots?"

The man says, "If that won't get the taste out, nothing will."

297.

You know you're getting old when you start having dry dreams and wet farts.

THE ONLY REASON THE PHRASE "LADIES FIRST" WAS INVENTED WAS SO GUYS COULD CHECK OUT WOMEN'S ASSES.

69% of people find something dirty in every sentence.

300.

The last time I was inside a woman was when I went to the Statue of Liberty.

301.

Why is it that when a man talks dirty to a woman it's sexual harassment, but when a woman talks dirty to a man it's $3.99 a minute?

302.

I ASKED MY WIFE WHY SHE NEVER BLINKED DURING FOREPLAY. **S**HE SAID SHE DIDN'T HAVE TIME.

303.

Life is sexually transmitted.

304.

THE DIFFERENCE BETWEEN A BOYFRIEND AND A HUSBAND IS ABOUT 45 MINUTES.

305.

If you don't believe in oral sex, keep your mouth shut.

306.

If a guy remembers the color of your eyes after a first date, chances are you've got small boobs.

307.

A GOOD BAR IS LIKE A GOOD WOMAN: LIQUOR IN THE FRONT AND POKER IN THE BACK.

308.

If sex is a pain in the ass,
then you're doing it wrong.

309.

I **LOVE EVERY BONE IN YOUR BODY, ESPECIALLY MINE.**

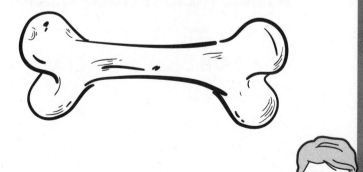

310.

Nice girls blush when they watch porn, good girls smile because they know they can do better.

311.

I WATCHED A REALLY SAD PORN FILM THE OTHER DAY. . . .

It was a real tear-jerker.

312.

Men are a lot like infants. If you want them to shut up, just put a boob in their mouth!

313.

I SHOULD HAVE KNOWN IT WOULD NEVER WORK OUT BETWEEN ME AND MY EX-GIRLFRIEND. . . .

After all, I'm a Pisces and she's a bitch.

314.

Men are like public toilets: the good ones are taken, and the rest are full of crap.

315.

IF A DOVE IS THE BIRD OF PEACE, THEN IS A SWALLOW THE BIRD OF LOVE?

316.

Virginity is like a soap bubble: one prick and it's gone.

317.

What's the difference between a slut and a bitch?

A slut is someone who'll have sex with anyone. A bitch is someone who'll have sex with anyone except you.

318.

A man walks into a bar.

As he sits down at the bar a busty blonde waitress pours him a drink and asks if he would like some food.

The man looks up at the menu above the bar and sees that it says, "Hot dog $2, Cheeseburger $5, Hand job $10."

He asks the waitress, "Are you the one who gives the hand jobs?"

She winks and replies, "Why, yes I am."

The man says, "Well in that case, wash your hands. I want a cheeseburger."

320.

Your finger fits right in it. You play with it when you're bored. Once you're married, you're stuck with the same one forever. What is it?

A ring.